Sing
With Robbie!

Exclusive distributors:
Music Sales Limited
8/9 Frith Street,
London W1D 3JB, England.
Music Sales Pty Limited
120 Rothschild Avenue
Rosebery, NSW 2018,
Australia.

Order No. AM969947
ISBN 0-7119-8799-8
This book © Copyright 2001 by Wise Publications

Music arranged by Jack Long
Music engraved by Paul Ewers Music Design

Cover design by Chloë Alexander
Photograph courtesy of London Features International

Printed in the United Kingdom by
Printwise (Haverhill) Limited, Suffolk.

Music Sales' complete catalogue describes thousands of titles and is
available in full colour sections by subject, direct from Music Sales Limited.
Please state your areas of interest and send a cheque/postal order
for £1.50 for postage to: Music Sales Limited, Newmarket Road,
Bury St. Edmunds, Suffolk IP33 3YB.

www.musicsales.com

Angels

Words & Music by Robbie Williams & Guy Chambers

told that sal - va - tion lets their wings

_____ un - fold.___ So when I'm

ly-ing in my bed, thoughts run-ning through my head, and I

feel that love is dead,— I'm lov - ing an - gels in - stead.

And through it all _____ she of - fers me— pro - tec -

- tion, a lot of love and af - fec - tion, whe-ther I'm right or

wrong. And down the wa - ter - fall,_____ wher-ev - er it___ may take___

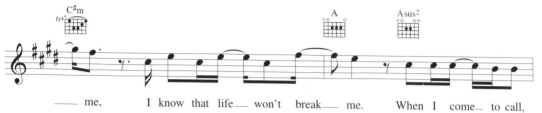

___ me, I know that life___ won't break___ me. When I come___ to call,

she won't for - sake___ me.

To Coda ⊕

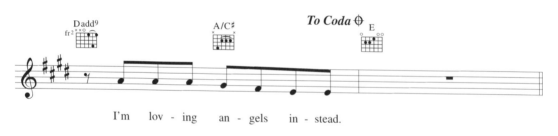

I'm lov - ing an - gels in - stead.

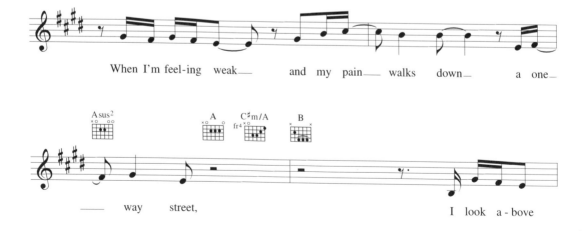

When I'm feel-ing weak___ and my pain___ walks down___ a one___

___ way street, I look a - bove

and I know— I'll al - ways be blessed

_____ with love.— And

as the feel-ing grows _____ she brings flesh to my bones. And

when love is dead I'm lov-ing an-gels in-stead. And through it all —

D.%. al Coda

◈ *Coda*

Instrumental

1.

2.

And through it all   all———— she of-fers me—— pro-tec-

-tion, a lot of love and af-fec - tion, whe-ther I'm right or

wrong. And down the wa - ter-fall,———— wher-ev-er it may take——

—— me, I know that life—— won't break—— me. When I come to call,

she won't for-sake—— me.

rit.

I'm lov - ing an-gels in-stead.

She's The One

Words & Music by Karl Wallinger

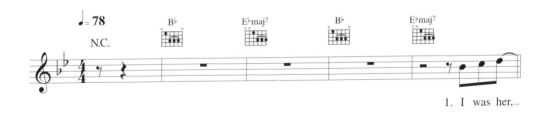

1. I was her,—

she was me, we were one,— we were free.—

Verses 3 & 4 see block lyric)

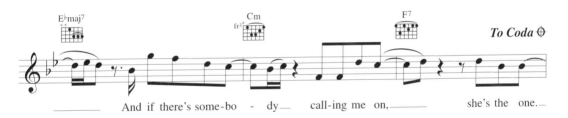

And if there's some-bo — dy— call-ing me on,— she's the one.—

If there's some-bo — dy— call-ing me on,—

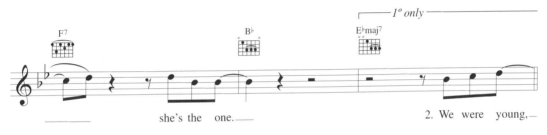

she's the one.— 2. We were young,—

we were wrong,_____ we were fun____ all a - long.

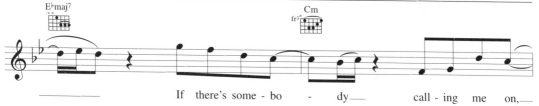

_____ If there's some - bo - dy___ call - ing me on,___

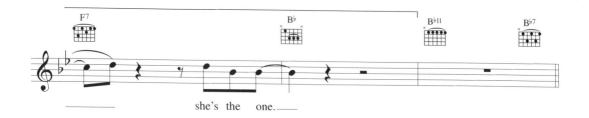

_____ she's the one.___

When you get to where you wan-na go,___ and you know the things you wan-na know,___ you're

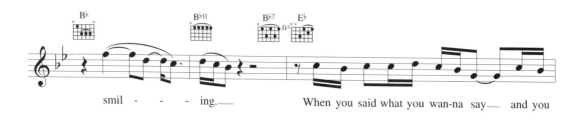

smil - - - ing.___ When you said what you wan-na say___ and you

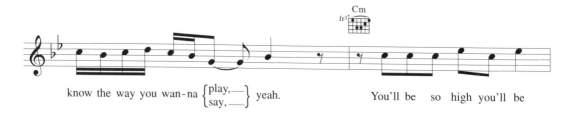

know the way you wan-na {play,___ / say, ___} yeah. You'll be so high you'll be

1. **2.**

D.%. al Coda

fly - - - ing. 3. Though the sea— -ing. 4. I was her,—

Coda

If there's some-bo - dy— call-ing me on,—

she's the one.— If there's some-bo -

- dy— call-ing me on,——— she's the one,——

rit.

she's the one.

Verse 3:
Though the sea will be strong
I know we'll carry on.
Cos if there's somebody calling me on, she's the one.
If there's somebody calling me on, she's the one.

Verse 4:
I was her, she was me
We were one, we were free.
And if there's somebody calling me on, *etc.*

11

Rock DJ

Words & Music by Robbie Williams, Guy Chambers,
Kelvin Andrews, Nelson Pigford & Ekundayo Paris

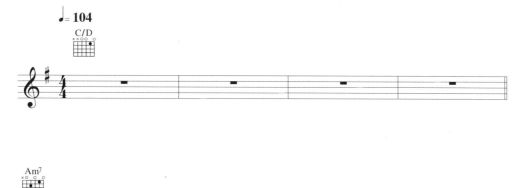

1. Me with the floor - show, kick - in' with your tor - so;
(Verse 2 see block lyric)

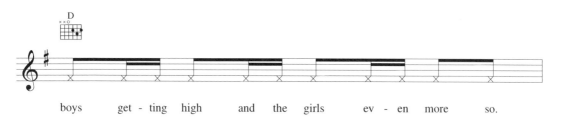

boys get - ting high and the girls ev - en more so.

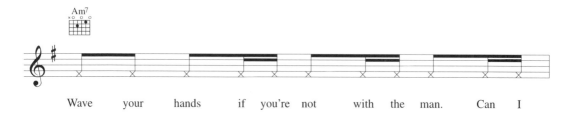

Wave your hands if you're not with the man. Can I

kick it? (Yes you can.) I got (funk), you got (soul),

we got ev - 'ry - bo - dy.   I've got the gift, gon-na stick it in the goal; it's

time   to   move your bo - dy.   Ba - by - lon back in bus -

- 'ness, can   I   get a wit - ness, ev - 'ry girl, ev - 'ry man.

____ (Ooh,   ooh,   ooh. ____) Hou - ston, do you hear ____

____ me? Ground con - trol, can you feel ____ me? Need per - mis - sion to   land. ____

____   I don't wan - na   rock, ___ D. J., ____ but you're

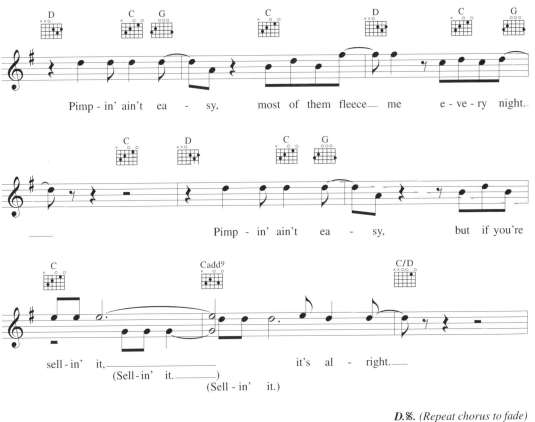

Pimp - in' ain't ea - sy, most of them fleece— me e - ve - ry night..

___ Pimp - in' ain't ea - sy, but if you're

sell - in' it,___ it's al - right.___
(Sell - in' it.___)
(Sell - in' it.)

D.%. (Repeat chorus to fade)

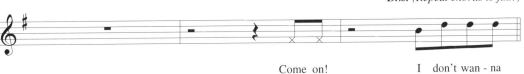

Come on! I don't wan - na

Verse 2:
Singin' in the classes
Music for the masses
Give no head no backstage passes
Have a proper giggle
I'll be quite polite
But when I rock the mike, I rock the mike (right)
You got no love then you're with the wrong man
It's time to move your body
If you can't get a girl but your best friend can
It's time to move your body.

I don't wanna be sleazy
Baby, just tease me
Got no family planned
Houston, do you hear me?
Ground-control, can you feel me?
Need permission to land.

I don't wanna rock *etc.*

15

Strong

Words & Music by Robbie Williams & Guy Chambers

♩ = 86

Ah,_____ ah,_____ ah._____

1. My breath smells of a thou-sand fags,___ and
(Verse 2 see block lyric)

when I'm drunk___ I dance like me Dad.___ I've

start-ed to dress___ a bit___ like him.___ And

ear-ly morn-ing, when I wake— up, I look like Kiss but with-out the make-up; and

that's a good line to take it to the bridge.——

And you know,— and you know— 'cos my life's a— mess,————

and I'm try-ing to grow._ So be-fore—— I'm old— I'll— con-fess.—

Play twice at D.%.

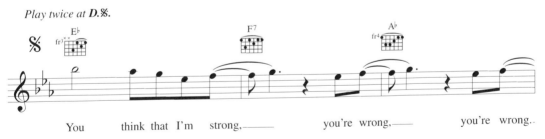

You think that I'm strong,——— you're wrong,—— you're wrong..

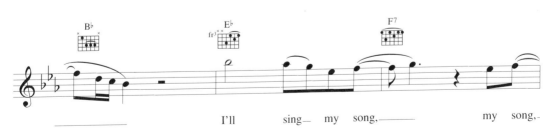

I'll sing— my song,——— my song,-

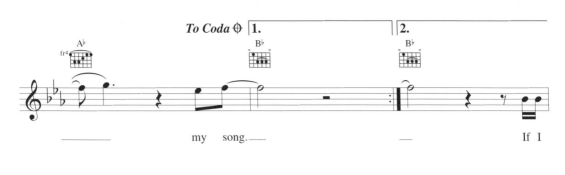

my song.—— — If I

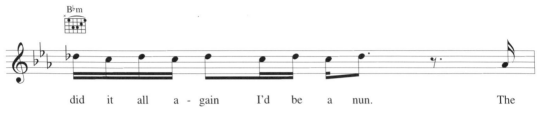

did it all a - gain I'd be a nun. The

rain was nev - er cold when I was young,—— I'm still young, we're still——

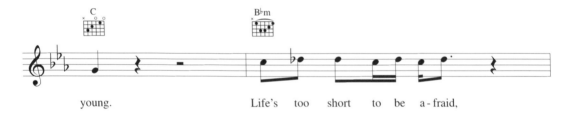

young. Life's too short to be a - fraid,

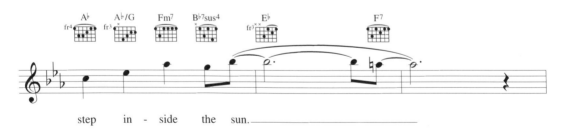

step in - side the sun.——

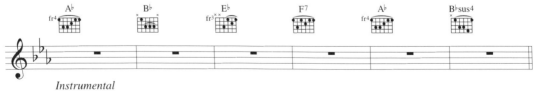

Instrumental

Fm7

And you know,— and you know— cos my life's a— mess,————

Fm7 **G♭6** **D♭add9**

D.%. al Coda

and I'm try - ing to grow.— Ah,———— hey,— hey.

Coda **B♭** **E♭**

———— Life's too short to be— a - fraid;—

F7

take a pill—— to numb the pain,

A♭ **B♭**

Repeat to fade

you don't have— to take the blame.————————

Verse 2:
My bed's full of takeaways
And fantasies of easy lays.
The pause button's broke on my video.
And is this real,
'Cos I feel fake?
Oprah Winfrey, Rikki Lake
Teach me things I don't need to know.
And you know, and you know
Cos my life's a mess,
And it's starting to show.
So before I'm old I'll confess.

You think that I'm strong *etc.*

Supreme

Words & Music by Robbie Williams, Guy Chambers,
Dino Fekaris & Frederick Perren

♩ = 96

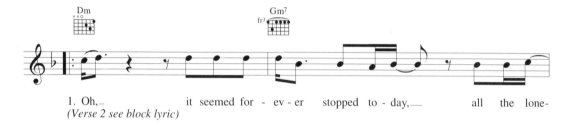

1. Oh,___ it seemed for - ev - er stopped to - day,___ all the lone-
(Verse 2 see block lyric)

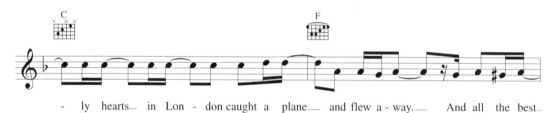

- ly hearts___ in Lon - don caught a plane___ and flew a - way.___ And all the best___

___ wo - men___ are mar - ried,___ all the hand - some men are gay,___ you feel de -

- prived.   Yeah,   are you ques - tion - ing___ your size?___   Is there a

tu - mour in —— your hu - mour, are there bags —— un - der your eyes? Do you leave

dents where — you sit, are you get - ting on —— a bit? Will you sur - vive? ——

—— You must sur - vive. —————— Where there's no ——

—— love in town —— this new cen - tu - ry —— keeps bring - ing you down. ——

—— All the pla - ces you have been —— try - ing to find —

To Coda ⊕ | **1.**

—— a love su - preme, —— a love su - preme. ——

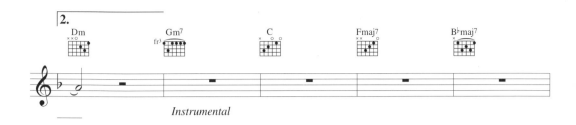

Instrumental

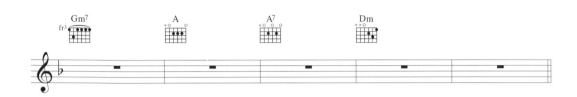

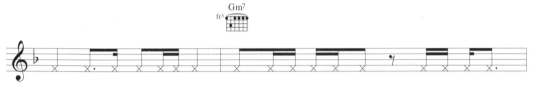

Spoken: I spy with my lit-tle eye some - thing be - gin-ning with. (ah) Got my back up,

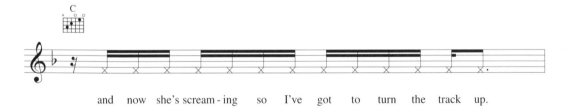

and now she's scream - ing so I've got to turn the track up.

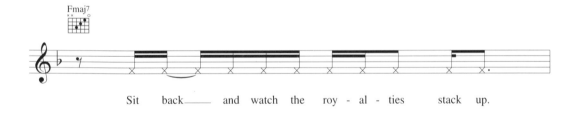

Sit back___ and watch the roy - al - ties stack up.

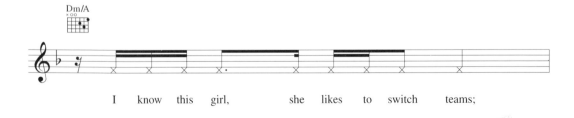

I know this girl, she likes to switch teams;

and I'm a fiend but I'm liv-ing for a love su-preme. When there's no____

⊕ *Coda*

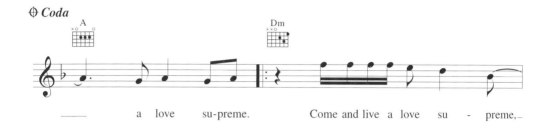

____ a love su-preme. Come and live a love su - preme,____

____ don't let it get you down,____

Repeat to fade

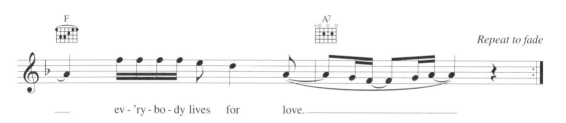

____ ev-'ry-bo-dy lives for love.____

Verse 2:
Oh, what are you really looking for?
Another partner in your life to abuse and to adore?
Is it lovey-dovey stuff?
Do you need a bit of rough?
Get on your knees.
Yeah, turn down the love songs that you hear
Cos you can't avoid the sentiment
That echoes in your ear
Saying love will stop the pain
Saying love will kill the fear
Do you believe?
You must believe.

When there's no love in town *etc.*

More great titles available in this series...

Sing With The Girls!
American Pie; Baby One More Time; Never Ever;
That Don't Impress Me Much; 2 Become 1.
Order No. AM969265

Sing With The Boys!
I Have A Dream; Livin' La Vida Loca; No Matter What;
She's The One; When You Say Nothing At All.
Order No. AM969276

Sing With Abba!
Dancing Queen; Mamma Mia; Money, Money, Money;
Waterloo; The Winner Takes It All.
Order No. AM969298

Sing Smash Hits!
Breathless; It Feels So Good; Oops!... I Did It Again;
Pure Shores; Sing It Back.
Order No. AM969287

...and other superb song collections for singers

Audition Songs for Female Singers 1
Don't Cry For Me Argentina...
plus Adelaide's Lament; Big Spender; Heaven Help My Heart;
I Can't Say No; I Will Survive; Out Here On My Own; Saving All My Love For You;
Someone To Watch Over Me; The Wind Beneath My Wings. ORDER NO. AM92587

Audition Songs for Female Singers 2
I Dreamed A Dream...
plus Another Suitcase In Another Hall; Fame; If I Were A Bell; Miss Byrd;
Save The Best For Last; Someone Else's Story; There Are Worse Things I Could Do;
What I Did For Love; You Can Always Count On Me. ORDER NO. AM950224

Audition Songs for Female Singers 3
Memory...
plus Can't Help Lovin' Dat Man; Crazy; Diamonds Are A Girl's Best Friend;
Now That I've Seen Her; Show Me Heaven; That Ole Devil Called Love;
The Winner Takes It All; Wishing You Were Somehow Here Again;
The Reason. ORDER NO. AM955284

Audition Songs for Female Singers 4
I Don't Know How To Love Him...
plus As Long As He Needs Me; Constant Craving; Feeling Good;
I Say A Little Prayer; If My Friends Could See Me Now;
It's Oh So Quiet; Killing Me Softly With His Song; Tell Me It's Not True;
You Must Love Me. ORDER NO. AM955295

Audition Songs for Female Singers 5
Chart Hits
Against All Odds (Take A Look At Me Now); American Pie; ...Baby One More Time;
Breathless; It Feels So Good; Man! I Feel Like A Woman; My Love Is Your Love;
Pure Shores; Rise; Sing It Back. ORDER NO. AM963765

Audition Songs for Female Singers 6
History Repeating; I Will Always Love You; Never Ever; Perfect Moment;
Search For The Hero; That Don't Impress Me Much; Torn; 2 Become 1;
What Can I Do; You Gotta Be. ORDER NO. AM963776

Audition Songs for Male Singers 1
Tonight...
plus All Good Gifts; Anthem; Being Alive; Corner Of The Sky; Funny;
High Flying, Adored; If I Loved You; Luck Be A Lady;
Why, God, Why? ORDER NO. AM92586

Audition Songs for Male Singers 2
Maria...
plus All I Need Is The Girl; Bring Him Home; Frederick's Aria;
I Don't Remember Christmas; Sit Down, You're Rocking The Boat;
Some Enchanted Evening; This Is The Moment; Where I Want To Be;
You're Nothing Without Me. ORDER NO. AM950213

Audition Songs for Kids
Any Dream Will Do; Consider Yourself; I'd Do Anything; No Matter What;
Spice Up Your Life; Thank You For The Music; The Candy Man; Tomorrow;
When I'm Sixty Four. ORDER NO. AM955273

ALL TITLES AVAILABLE FROM GOOD MUSIC RETAILERS OR,
IN CASE OF DIFFICULTY, CONTACT
MUSIC SALES LIMITED, NEWMARKET ROAD,
BURY ST. EDMUNDS, SUFFOLK IP33 3YB
TELEPHONE: 01284 725725; FAX: 01284 702592